Little Notes Necklace

by Roxanne & Sheryl - Stamp Studio

Roxanne & Sheryl *have been creating together for 7 years both in business and for fun. This inspired duo from* **Stamp Studio** *is always creating something new along with new ways to use eyelets, stamps, paper, fabrics and clay.*

Tuck tiny treasures, change for a phone call or a special love note into this charming bagin the color of a beautiful shimmering sea.

1. Cut two 3¼" squares of Blue suede.

2. Cut 1½" piece of tape, apply Gold leaf, attach to center of one suede piece.

3. Insert Gold eyelets and attach sea glass with wire.

4. Curl ends of wire into decorative spirals.

5. Attach suede pieces with Navy Blue eyelets.

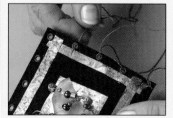

6. Sew Blue and Gold threads through eyelets.

7. Attach 24' to 36" of decorative threads/yarns for handle. Sew on beads.

Blue Suede Sea Glass Bag

MATERIALS: Blue Ultrasuede • 4 Gold and 13 Navy Blue eyelets • Gold leaf • Piece of sea glass • 24 gauge Gold wire • Blue and Gold Metallic thread • Decorative threads and yarns • Assorted beads • Round-nose pliers • ⅛" hole punch • Terrifically Tacky tape

INSTRUCTIONS: Cut two 3¼" squares of suede. Cut 1½" piece of 1" Terrifically Tacky tape. Peel off top layer and apply Gold leaf. Cut 4 Terrifically Tacky tape strips 3" x ¼" wide. Peel off top layer and apply Gold leaf. Peel off backing of 1½" piece and apply to center of one piece of Blue suede. Attach Gold eyelets where wire anchors sea glass. Wire sea glass to ultra suede stringing various beads on as you go. Pull leftover wire through last eyelet and curl in spirals. Apply strips of Gold leaf for a border. Fasten 2 pieces of Blue suede together using 5 Navy Blue eyelets per side. Weave Gold and Blue metallic threads through holes around edge. Cut 24" to 36" of various decorative threads and yarns. Thread ends through eyelets at top of bag from back to front, knot to secure. Leave 3" tails. Sew on beads.

Mica Tiles

by Gail Ellspermann

*M*ica tiles bring natural beauty to greeting cards made with colorful papers, eyelets and exciting rubber stamp images.

Gail Ellspermann *- Collage, cloth dolls, and art quilts are Gail's favorite forms of creative expression. A love of texture and color combined with a 20-year career as a professional floral designer are the foundation for her creative works. One of Gail's dolls won the Amateur Doll Division of the 2001 Sulky Challenge and Gail recently did extensive floral work on an award-winning 2002 Rose Parade float.*

Bee Good to Yourself Card

MATERIALS: $4\frac{1}{2}$" x 6" Sage Green notecard • $4\frac{1}{4}$" x $5\frac{1}{2}$" piece of Light Tan cardstock • $3\frac{3}{4}$" x 5" piece of vellum • 2" square Mica embossing tile • 4 Lavender and 4 Pink eyelets • Rubber stamps (*Impression Obsession* small leaf, *Stamp It!* flower, *PSX* bee and 'be good to yourself') • Vivid Tea Rose ink • Permanent Black ink • $\frac{1}{8}$" hole punch • Purple paper ribbon • Glue
INSTRUCTIONS: Using direct-to-paper method, smear Vivid Tea Rose ink on light Tan cardstock. Using Black ink , randomly stamp flower. Stamp corners of vellum with Black ink and small leaf stamp. Place vellum over card. Punch $\frac{1}{8}$" holes in corners, insert eyelets in holes and secure. Using $\frac{1}{8}$" hole punch, punch holes in corners of embossing tile. Place eyelets in holes and set. Stamp embossing tile with Black bee. Place embossing tile in center of vellum, pierce holes through paper and secure tile with ribbon. Stamp Black 'be good to yourself' on vellum. Glue Pink paper on card.

Pretty Face Card

MATERIALS: $3\frac{3}{4}$" x $8\frac{1}{2}$" Pale Pink notecard • 3" x 8" piece of White screen paper • Pink and White handmade paper • 3" x 6" Mica embossing tile • 6 Sage Green eyelets • Rubber stamps (*Impression Obsession* face, *Stampers Anonymous* large crackle) • Vivid Tea Rose and Black permanent ink • Dark Pink decorative yarn • $\frac{1}{8}$" hole punch • Pink and Blue pencils • Perfect Paper adhesive • Awl
INSTRUCTIONS: Stamp card with Black face. Subtly color lips and eyes using pencils. Tear pieces of Pink and White paper into random shapes. Glue on card. Stamp Vivid Tea Rose large crackle. Trim edges of screen paper and place over face. Punch $\frac{1}{8}$" holes in corners of embossing tile. Insert and set eyelets. Place embossing tile in center of card and use awl to punch holes through card. Weave yarn through eyelets and tie ends together inside card.

Party Dress Card

MATERIALS: 5" x 7" Pink card with torn edge • $4\frac{1}{4}$" x $5\frac{1}{2}$" piece of paper • $4\frac{1}{4}$" x $5\frac{1}{2}$" piece of Mica embossing tile • 6 White eyelets • Rubber stamps (*Inkadinkadoo* dress, *Impression Obsession* face) • Rose Red and Black ink pad • Clear embossing powder • Small piece of non-skid plastic placemat • Metallic Bronze paint • Pink cord • $\frac{1}{8}$" hole punch • Glue stick
INSTRUCTIONS: Ink the card using direct-to-paper method with Rose Red ink. Emboss with Clear embossing powder. Stamp Black dress. In upper right corner, stamp eyes using face stamp. Dab paint on small placemat piece and lightly stamp randomly on card. Cut tile into irregular shape. Attach tile to stamped paper with eyelets. Thread cord through holes. Glue paper on card with glue stick.

Painting Tip

To apply paint to tiny places, cut a small piece of plastic placement grid. Apply paint and press on paper.

Using this method allows you to apply as little as one speck of paint on a grid design.

Experiment! You'll really love the results.

1. Wipe color across cardstock with ink pad.

2. Apply the paint to placemat piece and press on stamped cardstock.

3. Attach the Mica tile with eyelets.

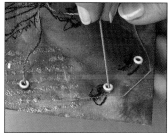

4. Sew cord through eyelets from front to back.

Vellum Night Lights

by Gail Ellspermann

1. Cut plastic cup in half with scissors.

2. Apply hearts to vellum, peel off protective film and pour beads into adhesive.

3. Attach vellum to plastic cup with eyelets.

*B*righten the night with color and whimsical or romantic designs. Night light shades are quick, easy and fun to make. Besides, we have so many to choose from!

Bumblebee Night Light Shade

MATERIALS: Night light • Clear plastic drinking cup • Yellow vellum • 8 Gold eyelets • Rubber stamps (*Stamp It* Black-eyed Susan and *Hero Arts* flying bee) • Black permanent ink pad • Black and White checked ribbon • Lace trim • Ultimate Bond tape • PopUp glue dot • 1/8" hole punch
INSTRUCTIONS: Cut plastic cup in half lengthwise. Cut Yellow vellum to fit over half cup adding 1/2" on all sides. Stamp Black-eyed Susan and Flying bee on vellum, let dry. Place vellum over plastic cup. Punch hole through cup and vellum in lower edge. Insert and set eyelet. Repeat for remaining eyelets. Trim vellum on all edges to conform to cup. Trim off lip of cup at bottom of shade. Weave ribbon through holes in lower and upper edges of shade. Cut half circle of Ultimate Bond tape to fit top of shade, remove White paper backing and stick to top of shade. Remove pink liner and cover top of shade with lace trim. Place large glue dot inside top of shade. Place shade on night light, press on top to secure to original night light cover.

Embossed Vellum Night Light Shade

MATERIALS: Night light • Clear plastic drinking cup • Embossed vellum • 8 Tan eyelets • Leaf charms • Gold jump rings • Upholstery trim scraps • Ultimate Bond tape • PopUp glue dot • 1/8" hole punch
INSTRUCTIONS: Cut plastic cup in half lengthwise. Cut embossed vellum to fit over half cup adding 1/2" on all sides. Place vellum over plastic cup. Punch hole through cup and vellum. Insert and set eyelet. Repeat for remaining eyelets. Trim paper on all edges to conform to cup. Trim off lip of cup for lower edge of shade. Attach leaves to lower eyelets using jump rings. Cut half circle of Ultimate Bond tape to fit top of shade. Remove White liner paper and adhere to top of shade. Remove Pink liner paper and cover top of shade with trim. Place large glue dot inside top of shade. Place shade on night light, press on top to secure to original night light cover.

Pansy Vellum Night Light Shade

MATERIALS: Night light • Clear plastic drinking cup • Susan Branch pansy vellum • 8 Pink eyelets • 28 gauge Red wire • Upholstery trim scraps • Ultimate Bond tape • PopUp glue dot • 1/8" hole punch

INSTRUCTIONS: Cut plastic cup in half lengthwise. Cut pansy vellum to fit over half cup adding 1/2" on all sides. Place vellum over plastic cup. Punch hole through cup and vellum. Insert and set eyelet. Repeat for remaining eyelets. Trim paper on all edges to conform to cup. Trim off lip of cup for lower edge of shade.

Cut three 24" pieces of Red wire. Wind 2 pieces through holes at lower edge of shade, wind 1 wire through holes at upper edge. Cut half circle of Ultimate Bond to fit top of shade, peel off White liner and adhere to top of cup. Remove Pink liner, cover with upholstery trim. Place large glue dot inside top of shade. Place shade on night light, press on top to secure to original night light cover.

Sparkly Hearts Night Light Shade

MATERIALS: Night light • Clear plastic drinking cup • Blue vellum • 8 Blue eyelets• Ultimate Bond hearts and tape• Pink Beedz • Leaf beads • Jump rings • PopUp glue dot • 1/8" hole punch

INSTRUCTIONS: Cut plastic cup in half lengthwise. Cut Blue vellum to fit over half cup adding 1/2" on all sides. Place sticky hearts on vellum. Remove Pink liner and apply Pink Beedz. Place vellum over cup. Punch hole through cup and vellum. Insert and set eyelet. Repeat for remaining eyelets. Trim paper on all edges to conform to cup. Trim off lip of cup for lower edge of shade. Cut half circle of Ultimate Bond tape to fit top of shade, peel off White liner and adhere to top of cup. Remove Pink liner, sprinkle with Pink Beedz. Use jump rings to add leaf beads to lower edge. Place large glue dot inside top of shade. Place shade on night light, press on top to secure to original night light cover.

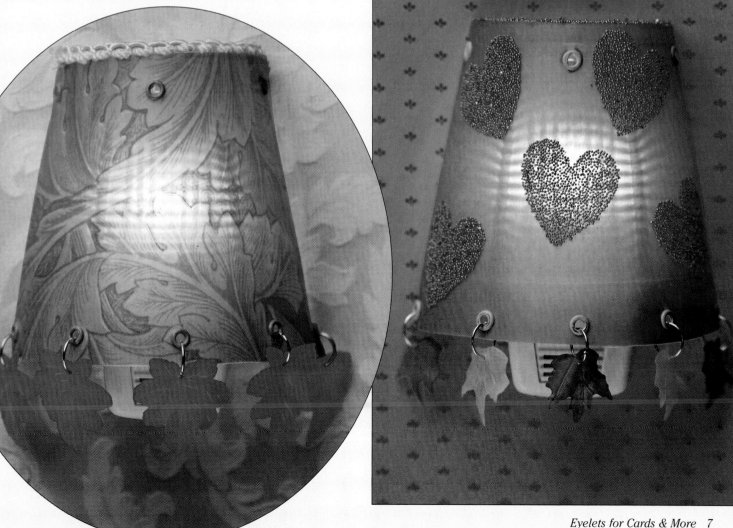

Tile Jewelry

by Gail Ellspermann

*M*ake jewelry and home accessories with a rich ethnic look. Combine unglazed stones, eyelets and rubber stamps to make a stunning fashion statement!

1. Wipe color across shapes with ink pad.

2. Stamp the design with Black ink.

3. Apply paint to placemat piece and press on shape.

4. Punch the holes and attach eyelets.

5. Thread the cord through the holes.

Stone Topped Box

MATERIALS: 3" round papier-mâché box • 6-sided irregular 2" piece of matboard • ³⁄₄" x 1" unglazed stone • 3 Sage Green eyelets • *Great Impressions* small leaf rubber stamp • Metallic Teal ink • Indigo and Sage ink • Clear embossing ink • Embossing powder (Powder Keg Carnivale, Gold, Clear) • Small piece of non-skid plastic placemat • Metallic Bronze paint • 22 gauge Metallic Green wire • ¹⁄₈" hole punch • Gold leafing pen • Awl • Heat gun

INSTRUCTIONS: Using direct-to-paper method, apply Indigo ink to stone. Use a heat gun to speed the drying. Stamp berry on stone with embossing ink, sprinkle with powder and heat.

Using direct-to-paper method, apply Sage ink to matboard. Stamp Black ink small leaf. Apply small amount of Bronze paint on small piece of placemat and tap lightly on matboard to transfer paint. Punch three ¹⁄₈" holes in matboard. Insert eyelets and set. Finish edge using leafing pen.

Apply Metallic Teal ink to papier-mâché box and lid. Emboss lid with Powder Keg Carnivale and box with Clear embossing powder. Place matboard on top of box and mark hole placement. Make holes with awl. Attach stone and matboard to top of box with wire.

Feather Rock Pin

MATERIALS: 1¹⁄₂" x 2" irregular 5-sided piece of matboard • 2¹⁄₂" irregular 6-sided piece of Pale Green cardstock • 2¹⁄₂" square of decorative paper • 1" x 1¹⁄₂" unglazed stone • 3 Sage eyelets • Rubber stamps (*Magenta* burst of dots, *PSX* feather, *JudiKins* small crackle) • Sage and Mandarin ink • Black permanent ink • Gold leafing pen • Adhesive pin back • 3 Gold jump rings • 3 Brass charms • ¹⁄₈" hole punch • Metallic Bronze paint • Small piece of non-skid plastic placemat • Orange colored pencil • Heat gun • Yes adhesive paste

INSTRUCTIONS: Using direct-to-paper method, smear matboard with Mandarin ink. Stamp Black burst of dots on matboard. Finish edge with leafing pen. Punch three ¹⁄₈" holes along lower edge. Insert and set eyelets. Use jump rings to attach charms.

Using direct-to-paper method, apply Sage ink to stone. Use heat gun to speed drying. Stamp Black feather on stone and color dots with pencil. Glue rock on matboard using paste. Stamp Black small crackle on cardstock. Apply paint to piece of placemat, lightly apply to paper. Let dry. Attach pin piece with paste. Attach adhesive pin back.

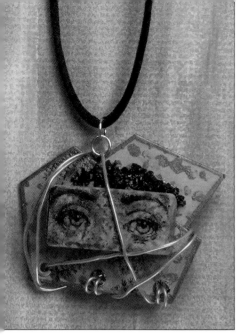

Looking at You Necklace

MATERIALS: 1½" x 2" and 1¾" x 2½" irregular pieces of matboard • Decorative paper to cover back of matboard • ¾" x 1½" unglazed stone • 3 Green eyelets • Rubber stamps (*Moon Rose* face, *JudiKins* fern) • Sage and Saffron ink • Black permanent ink • 22 gauge Gold wire • Obsidian Rox • Diamond Glaze • Copper leafing pen • Metallic Bronze paint • Small piece of non-skid plastic placemat • Black cord • 2 Gold jump rings • ⅛" hole punch • Yes adhesive paste

INSTRUCTIONS: Using direct-to-paper method, smear Sage ink on large piece and Saffron on small piece of matboard. Stamp Black fern on Sage piece. Place small amount of paint on piece of placemat and lightly tap on matboard pieces. Finish edges with leafing pen. Glue decorative paper to back of each matboard piece.

Using direct-to-paper method, smear Sage ink on stone. Use heat gun to speed drying. Stamp stone with Black eyes. Punch holes in bottom edge of Sage matboard piece. Insert and set eyelets. Attach layers with paste. Wind wire through eyelets and around matboard and stone. Be sure wires cross at top. Add jump rings at top for hanging cord. Place Diamond Glaze on edge of stone and sprinkle with Obsidian Rox.

Collage Necklace

MATERIALS: 1½" x 1¾" and 2¼" x 2½" irregular pieces of matboard • Decorative paper to cover back of matboard • ¾" x 1" unglazed tile • 3 Green eyelets • Rubber stamps (*Hero Arts* Italian poetry, *Stamp It* flower, *Impression Obsession* small leaf, *JudiKins* small crackle) • Ink pads (Mandarin, Saffron, Sage) • Permanent Black ink pad • Metallic Bronze paint • Small piece of non-skid plastic placemat • Flower charm • Gold jump ring • Gold leafing pen • Gold elastic • Black cord • ⅛" hole punch • Yes adhesive paste

INSTRUCTIONS: Using direct-to-paper method, smear one piece of matboard with Mandarin and the other with Saffron ink. On Mandarin piece, stamp Black Italian Poetry then stamp small crackle. On Saffron piece, stamp Black flower. Place a small amount of Bronze paint on placemat piece and pat on surface. Finish edges with leafing pen. Using direct-to-paper method, smear Sage ink on tile. Use heat gun to speed drying. Stamp Black small leaf on tile. Glue small piece of decorative paper on back of each matboard piece. Punch holes in matboard, insert and set eyelets. Attach layers with paste. Wrap with Gold elastic. Attach flower charm with jump ring. Insert jump ring in center top hole and add Black cord for necklace.

Serene Spirit Necklace

MATERIALS: 2" irregular piece of matboard • Decorative paper to cover back of matboard • 1¼" x 1½" unglazed stone • 3 Green eyelets • *Great Impressions* lady and fern rubber stamps • Mandarin and Saffron ink • Black permanent ink • Copper Rox • Diamond Glaze • Gold leafing pen • Metallic Bronze paint • Small piece of non-skid plastic placemat • Black cord • 3 Brass charms • 6 Gold jump rings • ⅛" hole punch • Heat gun • Yes adhesive paste

INSTRUCTIONS: Using direct-to-paper method, smear Mandarin ink on stone. Speed drying with heat gun. Stamp Black lady on stone.

Direct-to-paper ink matboard with Saffron ink. Stamp Black ferns. Place small amount of paint on piece of placemat and lightly tap on matboard. Punch one hole at top of matboard and 3 holes along bottom. Insert and set eyelets. Glue piece of decorative paper on back of matboard. Glue stone to matboard with paste. Place Diamond Glaze along sides of stone and sprinkle with Copper Rox. Use jump rings to attach charms to bottom of pendant. Insert jump rings in top of pendant and add hanging cord.

Bee Pin

MATERIALS: 2" x 2½" irregular piece of matboard • 2½" square of decorative paper • 1¼" x 1¾" unglazed oval stone • 4 Black eyelets • *PSX* bee stamp • Sienna ink • Black permanent ink • 22 gauge Dark Green wire • Copper Rox • Copper leafing pen • Diamond Glaze • Adhesive pin back • ⅛" hole punch • Small paintbrush • Yes adhesive paste

INSTRUCTIONS: Using direct-to-paper method, smear matboard with Sienna

ink. Glue piece of decorative paper to back. Finish edges with leafing pen. Stamp Black bee on small stone. Punch ⅛" holes in corners of matboard. Insert and set eyelets. Attach stone to matboard using paste. Cut two 18" pieces of wire. Insert wire through eyelet leaving 2" tail, go across and through eyelet on other corner. Twist end into a small spiral. Repeat for other piece of wire. Place Diamond Glaze along the edge of stone, sprinkle with Copper Rox, let dry. Paint entire piece with Diamond Glaze. Let dry. Attach pin back.

Belted Post-It Note Holder

MATERIALS: Two 4" squares of matboard • Two 5" squares of printed cover paper • Two 3½" squares of plaid liner paper • 3" x 6" piece of Off White suede paper • Post-It note pad • 4 Red large eyelets • Two 16" pieces of Red yarn • 3/16" hole punch • Perfect Paper adhesive

INSTRUCTIONS: Cover matboard with 5" paper square using paper adhesive. Trim paper across corner for neat corners. Fold suede paper in thirds lengthwise and fold to point at one end. Unfold, then secure each layer with paper adhesive. Let dry. Punch 4 holes in suede piece. Insert and set eyelets.

Glue 1¼" of square end of suede paper strip at the center inside of back cover. Glue plaid liner paper on inside of covers. Glue pointed end of strip across center of front cover, allowing 3/8" between covers when lying flat. Punch hole in center edge of back cover. Insert and set eyelet. Fold one piece of yarn in half, insert through eyelet and pass ends back through loop. Secure second piece of yarn to eyelet on suede paper tie. Insert note pad. Tie bow to close.

1. Glue paper on matboard with Perfect Paper.

2. Set eyelets in suede paper strip.

3. Glue end of ribbon to front cover of book.

4. Glue liner paper to center inside of covers.

Dragonfly Post-It Note Holder

MATERIALS: Two 4" squares of matboard • Two 5" squares of printed cover paper • Two 3½" squares of printed liner paper • 4" x 5" piece of Purple suede paper • Post-It note pad • 3 Blue large eyelets • 4½" of 1" Purple check ribbon • Silver dragonfly charm • 3/16" hole punch • Perfect Paper adhesive • Yes adhesive paste

INSTRUCTIONS: Cover matboard with 5" paper squares using paper adhesive. Trim paper across corner for clean, neat corners.

Fold suede paper in thirds lengthwise, then fold to point at one end. Unfold, then secure each layer with paper adhesive. Let dry. Punch 3 holes in suede paper strip. Insert and set eyelets.

Glue end of ribbon to inside of front cover. Glue square end of suede paper strip on center of inside back cover. Thread ribbon through eyelets. Trim end. Glue suede strip across center of front cover allowing 3/8" between covers when lying flat. Glue liner paper inside covers. Glue dragonfly with paste.

Booklet Ties

by Gail Ellspermann

*J*ournals are truly personal items filled with private thoughts, hopes and dreams. Decorate covers to make books as unique and outstanding as the words they contain!

Odonata Journal

MATERIALS: 6" x 9" journal • 5" x 8½" piece of decorative paper • 2" square and two 3½" x 7½" strips of Off White suede paper • 2 Black large eyelets • *Stampers Anonymous* Odonata dragonfly rubber stamp • Black permanent ink • 2 Gold dragonfly charms • Raffia • ³⁄₁₆" hole punch • Perfect Paper adhesive • Yes adhesive paste

INSTRUCTIONS: Stamp Black Odonata dragonfly on decorative paper.

Fold suede paper strips into thirds lengthwise. Fold each end into a point. Unfold then refold, securing each layer with paper adhesive. Punch hole in pointed ends. Insert and set eyelets. Fold and glue sides of suede square under ¼". Overlap square ends of suede strips, glue. Wrap and glue small suede piece to cover overlap.

Center journal on top of suede strip and glue strip to back of journal with paste. Bring ends to front of journal, thread 2 strands of raffia through each eyelet, tie bow. Tie charms to ends of raffia.

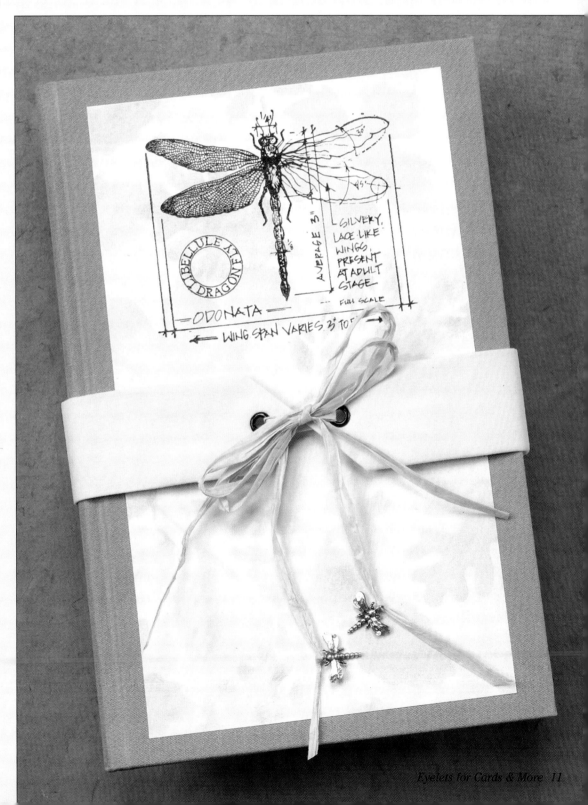

Vellum Soft

by pj dutton

pj dutton *has been creating samples for* **Judi-Kins** *for the past few years. She teaches across the country at conventions and rubber stamp stores and is a regularly featured artist in* THE RUBBER STAMPER, SOMERSET STUDIO *and* RUBBERSTAMPMADNESS.

Veritas

MATERIALS: Ultra Creme square card • Steel and Latte vellum • 4 Yellow eyelets • *JudiKins* rubber stamps (Italian script, architectural studies, Elizabeth, Veritas) • Brilliance Graphite Black and Coffee Bean ink • Fresco Mediterranean Tide and Golden Parchment ink pads • 1/8" hole punch • Deckle edge ruler
INSTRUCTIONS: Holding edge of ink pads on card surface, drag color across paper horizontally and vertically until you achieve the color and effect you like. Let dry. Stamp Coffee Bean Italian script on card front. Stamp Graphite Black architectural image on Steel vellum. Stamp Black Elizabeth and Veritas on Latte vellum. Using ruler, tear vellum to desired sizes. Place vellum on card, punch holes and attach with eyelets.

Harlequin

MATERIALS: Ultra Creme square card • Tea vellum • 4 Purple eyelets • Rubber stamps (*Stampers Anonymous* Harlequin scrap, *Acey Deucy* Giles) • Brilliance ink (Pearlescent Lime, Victorian Violet, Graphite) • 1/8" hole punch • Gold leafing pen • Assorted color pencils
INSTRUCTIONS: Stamp card front repeatedly with Harlequin scrap using Pearlescent Lime and Violet inks. Stamp Graphite Black ink Giles on vellum. Let dry. Color image on back of vellum. Trim to diamond shape. Edge vellum with leafing pen. Center vellum on card front, punch holes and attach with eyelets.

Beauty Desire Truth

MATERIALS: Ultra Creme tall card • Azure and Latte vellum • 12 Yellow eyelets • Rubber stamps (*JudiKins* pressed fern, *Stampers Anonymous* Truth, Desire and Beauty) • Brilliance ink pads (Pearlescent Jade, Pearlescent Orange, Pearlescent Yellow, Cosmic Copper) • 1/8" hole punch
INSTRUCTIONS: Drag ink pads directly across paper creating blocks of color. Stamp Pearlescent Jade ferns on colored areas. Cut vellum into rectangles and stamp words with Cosmic Copper ink. Arrange vellum on card front, punch holes and attach with eyelets.

Vellum Soft
by Gail Ellspermann

*Q*uickly and easily construct cards and a journal brimming with old world charm. All you need are rubber stamps, vellum, cardstock and eyelets.

Key Card

MATERIALS: 4¼" x 5½" Pale Tan notecard • 5½" square of Sage Green vellum • 3¾" x 5" piece of Black vinyl screen • 8 Green eyelets • Rubber stamps (*Hero Arts* Italian poetry, *Postmodern Design* keys, *JudiKins* keyholes) • Vivid Peach and Sienna ink • Permanent Black ink • ⅛" hole punch • Antique key • Sage Green ⅛" sheer ribbon • Glue

INSTRUCTIONS: Using direct-to-paper method, smear card with Vivid Peach ink and dab with Sienna. Stamp Black Italian poetry and keyholes.

Cut vellum into shape shown. Stamp Black keys along lower edge of vellum on back. Layer vellum over the screen and card. Punch ⅛" holes around vellum edges. Insert and set eyelets.

Punch holes in center of card on each side of antique key. Insert and set eyelets. Thread ribbon through eyelets and wrap ribbon around top of key to hold it in place. String end of ribbon to back of card and tie ends in knot.

Fern Journal

MATERIALS: 5" x 7" spiral bound journal • 4¼" x 5½" piece of cardstock • 3¾" x 4¾" piece of Moss Green lace paper • 3¼" x 4¼" piece of vellum • 4 Green eyelets • *Great Impressions* fern rubber stamp • Vivid Spring Green and Sage ink pads • Permanent Black ink pad • 4 small Brass washers • ⅛" hole punch • Perfect Paper adhesive

INSTRUCTIONS: Using direct-to-paper method, wipe cardstock with Vivid Spring Green, then Sage ink. Stamp Black fern randomly on cardstock. Stamp Black fern on back of vellum. Layer vellum over lace paper and cardstock. Punch holes in corners. Insert eyelet in small brass washer. Set eyelets. Glue the cardstock on front of journal to finish.

1. Wipe color on cardstock with ink pad.

2. Stamp the design with Black ink.

3. Place washers and insert eyelets to attach vellum to cardstock.

4. Glue cardstock on front of journal.

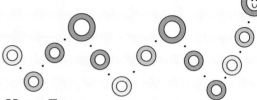

Sweet motifs, delicate colors and colorful eyelets make charming cards for all occasions.

Have Fun

MATERIALS: White notecard • Lime mat set • Assorted ⅛" eyelets • ³/₁₆" Meadow Green eyelets • *Simply Stamped* Have Fun rubber stamp • Black ink pad • ⅛" and ³/₁₆" hole punches • Fine-tip Black pen • Double-sided adhesive tape

INSTRUCTIONS: Attach Lime cardstock to card with tape. Place pattern on White cardstock and mark caterpillar placement. Use ³/₁₆" eyelets for head and humps. Punch holes using correct size punch. Insert and set eyelets. Stamp Have Fun and draw antennae with pen. Attach caterpillar notecard with tape.

Get Well

MATERIALS: White notecard • Apple Green mat set • 6 Black ⅛" eyelets • *Simply Stamped* Butterfly and Get Well rubber stamps • Black ink pad • Glitter Gel pens • Crystal lacquer • Black fine-tip pen • ⅛" hole punch • Double-sided adhesive tape

INSTRUCTIONS: Attach Green mat to card with tape. Stamp butterfly 3 times on White center mat. Punch holes, insert and set eyelets for antennae. Color in wings with gel pens. Let dry. Apply Crystal lacquer over bodies and wings. Let dry completely. Tape White mat to notecard with tape. Use Black pen to create dot trails. Stamp Get Well in upper right corner of card.

Bee Happy!

MATERIALS: White notecard • Small Sunflower mat set • Large sunflower eyelet • *Simply Stamped* Bee and Bee Happy! rubber stamps • Black permanent ink pad • 4" piece of heavy-duty Black thread • Scrap of white paper • Double-sided adhesive tape • ³/₁₆" hole punch • Glue

INSTRUCTIONS: Tape Sunflower mat to notecard. Attach eyelet to upper center part of paper. Stamp bee twice on a scrap of White paper. Cut around each border generously. Place 2 images back to back so bee will show on both sides. Line up bees and cut around edges leaving evenly spaced border. Place tape on back of one image. Place end of thread in glue before placing second cutout on top. Let dry. Thread hanging bee through eyelet hole. Tape down end of thread on back of center mat. Attach center mat to notecard. Stamp Bee Happy! at bottom center of center mat.

Have a Nice Day

MATERIALS: Tall Lime vellum mat set • Green vellum • Bristol White paper • Lime sparkles paper • ⅛" Lime Green eyelets • *Simply Stamped* Trio of flowers and Have a Nice Day rubber stamps • Black permanent ink pad • Foam mounting tape • Assorted fine-tip markers • ⅛" hole punch

INSTRUCTIONS: Tape Green vellum to notecard. Stamp trio of flowers several times along bottom of center mat. Color petals and grass with markers. Attach center mat to notecard. Stamp Have a Nice Day on White paper. Cut a slightly larger piece of Lime sparkles paper for mat. Use eyelets to attach papers. Tape message to notecard.

Lori Christensen is a stay-at-home mom who owns her own business, **Naptime Designs.** She designs all sample cards for **Simply Stamped** Papers & Rubber Stamps and teaches stamp classes at the **California Stampin'** store.

All American

MATERIALS: White notecard from Small Spring mat set • Platinum vellum • *Simply Stamped* USA T-shirt and all American rubber stamps • Black permanent ink pad • Scraps of Red, White and Blue paper • 1/8" eyelets (2 Red, 2 White, 2 Blue) • Foam mounting tape • 1/8" hole punch

INSTRUCTIONS: Cut 2 1/2" x 4" Platinum mat. Stamp T-Shirts on scraps of paper, cut out. Center vellum mat on notecard and attach eyelets 3/4" from top and bottom. Use foam mounting tape to attach T-shirts. Stamp All American at bottom center of notecard.

He's Here

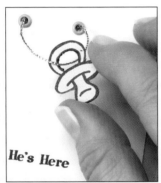

MATERIALS: Blue vellum mat set • Mint lined paper • Two Light Blue 1/8" eyelets • *Simply Stamped* Pacifier rubber stamp • Black permanent ink pad • Craft knife • 4" of Silver cord • Tape • Double-sided adhesive tape • 1/8" hole punch
INSTRUCTIONS:
Attach vellum using double-sided tape. Place adhesive toward center so it will not show through. Attach eyelets to top portion of White center mat. Stamp pacifier on small scrap of lined paper. Cut outside edge of image with scissors and use craft knife to cut away center of handle. Hang pacifier from cord. Thread both ends of cord through holes. Tape ends down on back of mat. Attach mat to notecard with double-sided tape.

For You

MATERIALS: Lime Sparkles window card • 3 spring color 1/8" eyelets • *Simply Stamped* Gift bag and For You rubber stamps • Black permanent ink pad • Watercolor pencils • 1/8" hole punch
INSTRUCTIONS: Stamp the gift bag in center of window. Color as desired. Punch random holes, insert and set eyelets. Stamp For You at the bottom center of card.

Celebrate

MATERIALS: Lavender Sparkles window card • White Sparkles paper • 4 Pink eyelets • *Simply Stamped* Cupcake and Celebrate! rubber stamps • Black permanent ink pad • Glitter gel pens • Crystal lacquer • 2 in 1 glue or double-sided tape • 1/8" circle and 2 square punches
INSTRUCTIONS: Select a square punch slightly larger than window and punch White Sparkles paper. With an even larger square, punch outside previous square to create a hollow frame. Place frame around window. Insert and set eyelets in corners of frame. Stamp Cupcake on a separate piece of paper and color with gel pens, let dry. Cover entire image with lacquer. Let dry completely. Cut out cupcake and glue or tape to center of window card. Stamp Celebrate! below framed window.

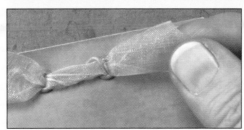

Gift Tag

MATERIALS: Wildflower Mini Vellum Foldover • 2 large Wildflower eyelets • 6" of 3/4" sheer Lavender ribbon • 3/16" hole punch
INSTRUCTIONS: Punch holes and secure eyelets near fold of tag. Thread ribbon from front to back then back to front. Trim ends.

Daisy Petal Card

MATERIALS: 4¼" x 5½" Cream notecard • 3½" x 5" piece of Pink handmade paper • 2½" x 4½" piece of torn Cream cardstock • Iridescent sparkle vellum • *Stamp Studio* Daisy petals rubber stamp • Fresco Vatican Wine ink pad • Black ink pad • Gold embossing powder • Embossing pen • Watercolor crayons • Heat gun • ³/₁₆" hole punch

INSTRUCTIONS: Stamp Black daisy petals on Cream cardstock and emboss. Stamp flower of daisy petals on vellum and emboss. Draw 2 petals on Cream cardstock with embossing pen, emboss. Color with crayons. Color flower with crayons. Cut around vellum petals close to center, but not all the way through. Keep all in one piece. Cut out 2 right side petals. Tear ½" of right side of card. Lightly sponge edge Vatican Wine. Tear edge of Pink mulberry paper. Stack paper pieces together on card and attach with ³/₁₆" eyelet through all layers.

1. Stamp entire design on cardstock and flower on vellum.

2. Color design with watercolor crayons.

3. Layer daisy pieces and attach to card with eyelet.

Hydrangea Bookmark

MATERIALS: 2½" x 5" glossy cardstock bookmark • Watercolor paper • Eyelets (Yellow, Periwinkle, Plum, Eggplant, Fuchsia) • *Stamp Studio* Potted heart rubber stamp • Black ink pad • Watercolor pencils • 18" of 1" Purple sheer ribbon • ⅛" hole punch

INSTRUCTIONS: Stamp Black potted heart on watercolor paper. Color with pencils. Stamp top flower 5 times on watercolor paper and color with various Blues, Purples and Pinks. Glue potted heart on glossy cardstock. Cut out flowers and lightly glue each one around center flower on bookmark. Secure flowers with eyelets. Tie ribbon through top and trim ends.

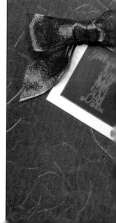

Garden Greetings Card

MATERIALS: 4¼" x 5½" Sage Green notecard • 3" square of Sage Green and scrap of White handmade paper • Scrap of White cardstock • 2 Vanilla Bean and 4 Fern Green eyelets • *Stamp Studio* Rubber stamps (grape swirl, dragonfly, Garden Greetings) • Purple and Green brush markers • Embossing ink pad • Glitter embossing powder • Heat gun • ⅛" hole punch • Glue

INSTRUCTIONS: Stamp grape swirl in corners of card using brush markers to color stamp. Stamp and emboss dragonfly on White cardstock and cut out. Stamp and emboss Garden Greetings on White handmade paper. Glue square on card diagonally and attach Garden Greetings with eyelets. Attach dragonfly above Garden Greetings. Place Fern Green eyelet in the center of each grape swirl vine.

Thank You Banner   by pj dutton

MATERIALS: Glossy White and Shimmer White cardstock • 8 Metallic Blue eyelets Copper eyelet washers • *Stampers Anonymous* alphabet stamps • Inks (Kaleidacolor Blue Breeze, Brilliance Cosmic Copper) • Brayer • Ruler • Craft knife • ⅛" hole punch • Copper leafing pen • Double-sided tape

INSTRUCTIONS: Stamp Copper letters on Glossy White cardstock. Let dry. Brayer over letters with Kaleidacolor ink pad. Cut letters using a ruler and craft knife into 1½" squares. Edge squares with Copper leafing pen. Cut White cardstock into 2" squares and attach letters using double-sided tape. Punch holes using hole guide. Attach squares with eyelet washers and eyelets. Always add next letter under previous letter so banner will fold properly.

To make hole guide, cut a square of cardstock. Measure and punch holes in one corner of square. Use this as a guide when punching holes. Line up corner and punch. This way all of the holes will be evenly punched.

Forget Me Not Card

MATERIALS: 4¼" x 5½" White notecard • 3½" x 4¼" piece of sparkle vellum • 2 Pink eyelets • *Stamp Studio* Forget Me Not rubber stamp • Black ink pad • Watercolor crayons • ⅛" hole punch
INSTRUCTIONS: Stamp Forget Me Not on card. Color with watercolor crayons. Attach vellum over Forget Me Not with eyelets.

Hanging Double Heart

MATERIALS: 4¼" x 5½" White notecard • Watercolor paper • 2 White eyelets • *Stamp Studio* Hanging heart rubber stamp • Black ink pad • Watercolor crayons • 12" of ¼" sheer ribbon • ⅛" hole punch • Double-sided tape
INSTRUCTIONS: Stamp hanging heart twice on watercolor paper. Color with watercolor crayons. Cut out around images and inside heart hanger. Attach 2 White eyelets to cardstock and tie hanging hearts with thin ribbon. Attach hearts to card with tape.

Daisy Square Card

MATERIALS: 4¼" x 5" Sage Green card • Paper (2¾" White watercolor , 3½" White dot embossed cardstock , 3" Pink vellum) • 4 White ³⁄₁₆" and 5 Pink ⅛" eyelets • *Stamp Studio* Daisy square rubber stamp • Black ink pad • Watercolor crayons • ⅛" and ³⁄₁₆" hole punch
INSTRUCTIONS: Stamp daisy square on watercolor paper. Crayon Pink and Yellow petals and Bright Green around edge giving the tiny flowers a touch of Pink. Cut irregular edges. Stack squares on card, attach center of daisy with Pink eyelet. Attach dot paper first with White ³⁄₁₆" eyelets and then ⅛" inch eyelet in center.

*F*lowers, clothing and heart designs grace these feminine cards with the freshness of love and springtime!

La Petit Card

MATERIALS: 4¼" x 5½" White embossed notecard • Watercolor paper • 3 Silver and 2 White eyelets • *Stamp Studio* La Petit rubber stamp • Black ink pad • Watercolor crayons • 27" of Iridescent cord • ⅛" hole punch • Glue
INSTRUCTIONS: Stamp La Petit 3 times on watercolor paper. Color with crayons. Cut out. Lightly glue 3 across card. Attach a Silver eyelet in the hanger of each jacket. Thread ribbon through eyelets and tie bow. Tear out 'La Petit', lightly watercolor and attach with White eyelets.

Hanging Single Heart

MATERIALS: 4¼" x 5½" Peach embossed notecard • Watercolor paper • Cardstock (2½" x 3¼" Pink print, 2¼" x 2¾" White corrugated) • 4 Pink and 2 White eyelets • *Stamp Studio* Hanging heart and Happy Valentine's Day rubber stamps • Black and Pink ink pads • Watercolor pencils and crayons • 12" of ¼" White sheer ribbon • ⅛" hole punch • Double-sided tape
INSTRUCTIONS: Stamp hanging heart on watercolor paper. Color with watercolor pencils and crayons. Cut out around image and inside hanger. Place cardstock pieces on card and attach with Pink eyelets. Attach White eyelets to upper corner of White corrugated paper. Tie on hanging heart with ribbon. Stamp Pink 'Happy Valentine's Day' on card.

Dance the Dream

MATERIALS: 4¼" x 5½" White notecard • Watercolor paper • 2⅝" square of Blue mulberry paper • Silver eyelet • *Stamp Studio* Fancy dress and Dance the Dream rubber stamps • Black ink pad • Metallic Silver ink pad • Watercolor pencils • ⅛" hole punch • Double-sided tape
INSTRUCTIONS: Stamp fancy dress on watercolor paper and color with watercolor pencils. Cut out around image. Center on mulberry paper and attach to front of card with eyelet. Stamp 'Dance the Dream' on bottom of card with Silver Encore Metallic Pad.

*E*arth colors and snappy shapes make delight-ful cards that everyone will appreciate!

Dog with Collar

MATERIALS: Beige cardstock • Beige tag • Paper (scraps of White, Black and Brown, 1" x 1¾" Red, 3¼" x 4¼" Brown print) • 5 Gold eyelets • Punches (⅛" circle, ½" heart, ¼" circle, ⅝" egg) • Sponge • Light Brown ink • Small heart charm • Wire or jump ring • Glue

INSTRUCTIONS: Cut Beige paper to 5½" x 8½", fold in half to make card. Mount Brown paper on card. On end of tag, cut half way down center. Fold strips to form dog ears. Trim ends with scissors. Sponge around face area with ink. Punch White ovals and Black circles for eyes and Brown heart for nose. Glue heart over tag hole. Glue eyes in place. Punch 5 holes in Red paper, insert eyelets and secure. Attach heart charm with wire or jump ring. Glue dog head and collar together and mount on card.

Shopping Bag

MATERIALS: 4¼" x 5½" Cream notecard • Brown and Red cardstock • 2¾" x 3¾" piece of embossed Red paper • 2 Beige eyelets • Embossing ink pad • Gold embossing powder • Beige crinkles or corrugated strips • *Hero Arts* heart stamp • Red rhinestone • ⅛" hole punch • Mini zig zag scissors • Mounting tape

INSTRUCTIONS: Mount Red paper on card. Cut Brown cardstock into shopping bag and trim top with zig zag scissors. Cut narrow strip for handle. Fold and attach bag with eyelets as shown. Emboss Gold heart on Red cardstock and cut out. Attach with mounting tape for dimensional effect. Attach bag to Red paper with mounting tape. Secure rhinestone with glue. Stuff crinkles into bag.

Metallic Stars

MATERIALS: 4¼" x 5½" textured Ivory notecard • Metallic Gold printed paper • Paper (2⅞" x 4⅜" Gold, 3" x 4½" Copper) • 2 Gold and 2 Copper eyelets • Copper foil • 1¼" and 2" star punches • Gold wire • Copper tape • 1¼" x 4¾" piece of window screen mesh • ⅛" hole punch • Double-sided tape

INSTRUCTIONS: Glue Copper and Gold paper on card. Punch stars from printed paper and Copper foil. Attach mesh to card with Copper tape. Lightly secure stars with double-sided tape and punch holes for eyelets. Attach eyelets. Slip wire through larger star, twist and curl into long springs. Mount on card.

Dog Pattern
Fold ears down

Bag Pattern

Tree Patterns

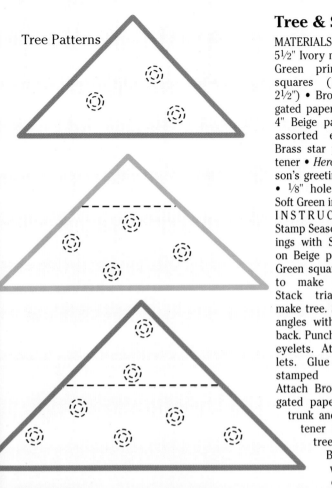

Tree & Star

MATERIALS: 4¼" x 5½" Ivory notecard • Green print paper squares (1¾", 2", 2½") • Brown corrugated paper • 3¼" x 4" Beige paper • 12 assorted eyelets • Brass star paper fastener • *Hero Arts* Season's greetings stamp • ⅛" hole punch • Soft Green ink • Glue

INSTRUCTIONS: Stamp Season's Greetings with Soft Green on Beige paper. Fold Green squares in half to make triangles. Stack triangles to make tree. Secure triangles with tape on back. Punch holes for eyelets. Attach eyelets. Glue tree on stamped paper. Attach Brown corrugated paper for the trunk and star fastener on top of tree. Glue Beige paper with tree on card.

Tic-Tac-Toe

MATERIALS: 4¼" x 5½" Ivory notecard • Brown wood paper • 4 Beige eyelets • X and O from alphabet stamp set • Gold ink pad • Gold embossing powder • ⅛" hole punch • Glue dots

INSTRUCTIONS: Cut thin strips of wood paper. Arrange in tic-tac-toe grid. Carefully punch holes, wood paper splits easily, so do not make strips too narrow. Attach eyelets. Place on Ivory card and stamp X's and O's with Gold ink. Remove grid and emboss X's and O's. Attach tic-tac-toe grid with glue dots.

Tag with Yarns

MATERIALS: 4¼" x 6" Tan embossed notecard • 3" x 4½" piece of Black paper • 3" x 5" piece of 2-tone Beige paper • 2 Beige eyelets • Small Brown tag • Gold and Black ink • *Hero Arts* Manuscript and postage rubber stamps • Decorative yarns • ⅛" hole punch • Paper embossing tool • Glue

INSTRUCTIONS: Randomly stamp manuscript and postage stamps with Gold ink on Black paper. Mount on notecard. Stamp Brown tag with Black and Gold postage stamps. Attach decorative yarns to tag. Paper emboss Beige 2-tone paper and fold as shown for pocket. Attach eyelets. Glue pocket on Black paper. Tuck tag into pocket.

Tag Pattern

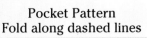
Pocket Pattern
Fold along dashed lines

Sally Traidman designs for **Hero Arts** and other rubber stamp and paper companies. She owns her own retail mail order business... **Rubberstampler.**

Colorful Cars

MATERIALS: 5½" x 8½" piece of cloud paper • Asphalt and grass printed paper • Paper scraps (Green, Yellow, Blue, Orange, Hot Pink, Purple) • 12 assorted eyelets to match paper scraps • ⅛" circle and 1" car punches • White colored pencil • Glue stick

INSTRUCTIONS: Fold cloud paper in half for card. Cut wavy road and grass from printed papers and glue on cloud paper. Draw traffic line with White pencil. Punch cars from scraps of paper and attach to card with matching eyelets. Glue cars on road.

Birthday Ribbons

MATERIALS: Cardstock (5½" x 8½" Pink, 4" x 5" Purple, 3¾" x 4¾" Green, 3½" x 4½" Yellow, 3¼" x 4¼" Black) • Printed birthday ribbon (Green, Purple, Pink) • 6 eyelets to match ribbon • ⅛" hole punch • Glue stick

INSTRUCTIONS: Fold Pink cardstock in half for card. Cut ribbons to equal lengths and trim to point. Lightly secure each ribbon on Black cardstock with glue stick so they do not move. Punch holes and insert matching eyelet in each end. Secure eyelets. Layer and glue cardstock on card as shown.

 Ribbon Pattern

Flowers in the Grass

Grass Pattern

MATERIALS: 5½" x 8½" textured White notecard • Scraps of paper (Green, Pale Green, Pink, Lavender, Purple, Rose) • 5 Yellow eyelets • Punches (⅛" circle, 1" flower, 1¼" flower) • Glue stick

INSTRUCTIONS: Randomly cut Green and Pale Green paper into long irregularly shaped triangles. Glue on White card. Punch out the flower shapes. Punch holes in the flower centers and attach with eyelets. Glue the flowers on card between blades of grass.

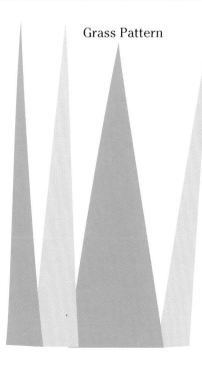

A new car, a special birthday, the birth of a child, a simple act of kindness, a beautiful spring day… all of these are reasons for joy and celebration

No Act of Kindness

MATERIALS: 4¼" x 5½" Pale Blue notecard • Paper (2" x 4" Sage Green, 2½" x 5½" Ivory) • 2 Green eyelets • *Hero Arts* Kindness and circle twirl rubber stamps • Sage Green ink pad • Embossing ink pad • Gold embossing powder • ⅝" Ivory sheer ribbon • ⅛" hole punch • Glue stick

INSTRUCTIONS: Randomly stamp circle twirl stamp all over notecard. Emboss 'Kindness' stamp on Sage Green paper. Punch holes and attach Sage Green eyelets. Knot ribbon in top eyelet and run ribbon down behind paper to come out bottom eyelet, knot. Trim ends. Mount on Ivory and then on card.

Flowers Hello

MATERIALS: 4¼" x 6" Cream feather notecard • White and Green paper • 3 eyelets to match flowers • Rubber stamps (*Rubberstampler* sunny hello, *Hero Arts* large shadow and flower) • Soft Leaf and Black ink pads • Duo-Daubers (Pink, Yellow, Lavender) • Leaf and ⅛" circle punches • Glue stick

INSTRUCTIONS: Cut 3" x 3½" White rectangle. Stamp Soft Leaf shadow. Ink flower stamp with Duo-Daubers and stamp on White paper. Cut out close to edges leaving slight White edge. Punch Green leaves. Arrange flowers and leaves on shadow area. Attach flowers with eyelets. Mount White paper on card. Stamp Black sunny hello.

Checkerboard Flowers

MATERIALS: Sage Green tall notecard • White paper • Green cord • 12 eyelets to match paper backgrounds • *Hero Arts* checkerboard and fresh flowers rubber stamps • Stamp pads (Lavender, Green, Rose, Black) • Colored pencils • 3 Purple 4mm beads • ⅛" hole punch • Glue stick

INSTRUCTIONS: Stamp Lavender, Rose and Green checkerboards on White paper. Trim leaving narrow White edges. Stamp Black flowers and color with pencils. Punch holes in corners and attach eyelets. Punch 2 tiny holes at top of card. String cord through eyelets starting at bottom. When you get to top, slip cord through first hole, come up through back, attach tiny bead, go down again to back and come up again down other side. Attach 2 tiny beads at each end with knots. Lightly secure checkerboards on card.

Baby Congratulations

MATERIALS: 4¼" x 5½" White notecard • White flannel paper • Paper (3¾" x 4¾" Blue, 3½" x 4½" Blue gingham, Blue scrap, Pale Blue scrap) • 6 Blue eyelets • *Rubberstampler* congratulations rubber stamp • Black ink • Punches (⅞" bow, ⅛" circle, ¼" circle, ⅝" circle) • Glue stick

INSTRUCTIONS: Cut baby onesie from White flannel paper. Punch holes and attach eyelets. Glue onesie on gingham paper. Punch bow and circles from Blue papers to make rattle, glue on corner. Stamp Black congratulations on tiny piece of White paper and glue in place. Assemble card as shown.

Here is a unique collection of wonderful designs to bring out the creativity of any crafter!

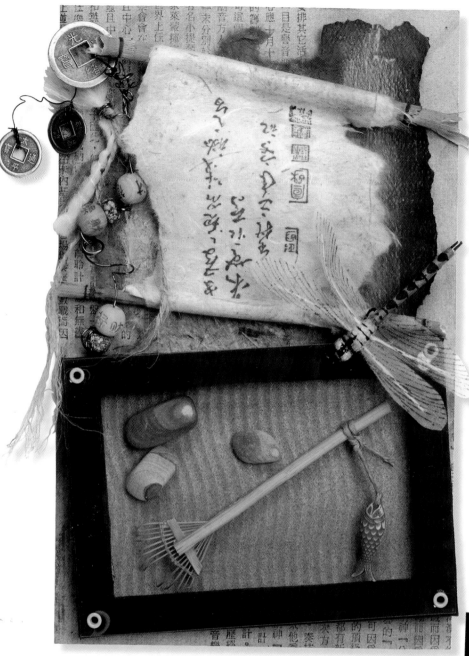

by Tim Holtz

Asian Sand Garden

MATERIALS: 5½" x 8½" piece of Sage Green cardstock • Mulberry paper (Rust, Tan, White) • Scrap of decorative paper • 4 Green eyelets • 3 *Hero Arts* Asian script rubber stamps • Brown and Black ink pads • Two 5" pieces of bamboo • 4" x 6" piece of sandpaper • Black foamcore • 3⅝" x 5¼" piece of acetate • Small stones • Mini sand rake • 3 wood 10mm beads • 2 glass beads • Dragonfly and Asian fish charms • 3 Asian coins • 24 gauge Green wire • Natural jute • • Decorative yarn • Paper crimper • Craft knife • Glue

INSTRUCTIONS: Stamp Brown Asian script on White mulberry paper for scroll. Stamp Black script on cardstock. Form around bamboo. Run sandpaper through paper crimper and trim to 3⅝" x 5¼".

Cut two 3⅝" x 5¼" pieces of foamcore for frame. Cut opening leaving ½" border. Glue pieces together and sandpaper on bottom. Tie fish bead to rake handle with jute. Glue stones and rake on sandpaper. Attach acetate to frame with eyelets.

Tear and glue mulberry and decorative paper on cardstock. Glue frame and scroll in place. Twist wire around jute and decorative yarn. Add beads and coins to wire, twisting wire to secure. Glue on cardstock. Glue dragonfly on frame.

Travel the world, even if only in your mind, with these very pleasingly different designs!

by Roxanne & Sheryl - Stamp Studio

From the Beach Card

MATERIALS: 4¼" x 5½" Dark Blue cardstock • 3¾" x 5" piece of Blue and Gold decorative paper • Medium Manila tag • 8 Gold eyelets • *Stamp Studio* From the beach rubber stamp • Blue ink pad • Small bottle • Small shell • Blue seed beads • Assorted seed and E beads • 24 gauge Gold wire • 18" of ¼" Ivory sheer ribbon • ⅛" hole punch

INSTRUCTIONS: Fill bottle with seed beads and seashell. Cut an 18" piece of 24 gauge Gold wire and wrap around neck of bottle 2 or 3 times. On bottom of tag, stamp 'from the beach'. Attach decorative paper to cardstock with eyelets. Attach tag to cardstock with eyelet though tag hole. Attach eyelet just above tag. On top half of tag place 2 eyelets ½" apart horizontally. Attach tiny bottle by running wire through eyelets and twisting on back and then running wire back up through front. Slide assorted beads on wire and wrap around paintbrush to curl. Tie bow through eyelets at top of tag.

by Tim Holtz

Journal

MATERIALS: 5" x 7" blank journal • Gold Bravissimo paper • 4⅜" x 5¼" and 1⅛" x 3" pieces of Black cardstock • 4⅜" x 5¼" and ⅝" x 2½" pieces of Manila paper • Manila shipping tag • Old postcard • 8 Silver eyelets • *Stampers Anonymous* rubber stamps (eye, travel, journal) • *Limited Edition* Mini word tiles • Ink pads (Brown, Black, Moss Green) • Black embossing powder • Piece of a CD • Rusty key • Gold leaf • Leaf adhesive • Gold leafing pen • Hemp • Green decorative yarn • 2 Silver melon beads • Heat gun • ⅛" hole punch • Glue stick

INSTRUCTIONS: Cover journal with Gold paper. Color edges of journal paper with leafing pen. Wrap 6 strands of hemp around journal and knot ends together. Tie in a knot for closure. Tie on key with hemp.

Apply leafing adhesive to piece of CD, let dry, then apply Gold leaf. Stamp vision eye stamp and emboss.

Rub Green ink lightly over shipping tag and Manila paper. Stamp Brown travel images. Tear bottoms of Manila and large piece of cardstock. Attach Manila paper to cardstock with eyelets. Tear postcard. Thread yarn through top of tag. Tie on beads and secure with knots. Glue postcard pieces, tag, CD piece and scrabble tiles as shown. Glue cardstock on front of journal.

Stamp Brown journal on small piece of Manila paper, glue on small cardstock. Attach eyelets to corners and glue on journal.

Journals are a terrific way to remember your travel experiences or to record your daily thoughts and ideas.

Tim Holtz *has been crafting his entire life. He is the creative consultant for* **Ben Franklin Crafts** *store in Prescott, Arizona. He teaches workshops on stamping and much more. His creativity incorporates a variety of elements and techniques from many types of crafts.*

Southwest Card

MATERIALS: 4¾" x 7" Tan card • Bravissimo papers (3⅝" x 4½" patina, 4¼" x 5¼" suede, 7" x 9½" snakeskin) • Scraps of Tan and Turquoise paper • 3¼" x 4" piece of denim • 8 Copper eyelets • Adios and Southwestern figures rubber stamp • Black ink • Clear embossing ink • Antiquities embossing powders • Metallic paints • Small paintbrush • Tiny turquoise pieces • 2 Turquoise disks • Lizard charm • Denim fibers • ⅛" hole punch • Glue

INSTRUCTIONS: Paint denim with metallic paints and emboss with powders and Clear embossing ink. Stamp figures with Black ink. Use eyelets to layer and fasten denim to patina and suede papers. Cover card with snakeskin paper. Stamp Adios on Tan scrap, trim sides and tear ends. Glue on Turquoise scrap and tear Turquoise edges.

Glue Turquoise paper on denim and layered papers on card. Glue lizard and Turquoise pieces in place. Fold denim fibers in half and tie knot. Glue on side of card. Tie Turquoise disks on ends of fibers.

Imaginations

*D*ream,
Imagine,
Inspire...
the artist in all of us
comes to life in these
clever pieces.

by Gail Ellspermann

Inspire Art Pin

MATERIALS: 2¼" irregular 5-sided piece of matboard • ½" x 1¼" plastic rectangle • Scrap of White cardstock • Decorative paper to cover back of matboard • Gold eyelet • Rubber stamps (inspire, ART) • Ink pads (Black, Green, Orange, Teal) • Brass corner charm • Metallic Teal and Gold paint • Small piece of non-skid plastic placemat • Copper Rox • Gold leafing pen • Self-adhesive pin back • ⅛" hole punch • Glue

INSTRUCTIONS: Color matboard Teal, cardstock Green and rectangle Orange. Stamp Black inspire on cardstock and ART on rectangle. Color edges of rectangle with leafing pen. Tear around edges of cardstock. Glue decorative paper on back of matboard and finish edges with leafing pen.

Insert eyelet in corner and glue pieces as shown. Attach pin to back.

Dream Pin

MATERIALS: Small Cream tag • Scrap of White cardstock • Gold eyelet • Rubber stamps (Dream, globe, eye) • Ink pads (Black, Sage Green, Rainbow) • 1¼" hexagon unglazed tile • 12" of ⅝" Green ribbon • 22 gauge Red wire • Round-nose pliers • Gold fibers • Gold leafing pen • Self-adhesive pin back • ⅛" hole punch • Glue
INSTRUCTIONS: Color tag and cardstock with Rainbow ink pad. Stamp Black globe on tag and 'Dream' on cardstock. Tear around cardstock and attach to tag with eyelet.

Color hexagon Sage Green and stamp Black eye. Color edges with leafing pen.

Coil ends of wire and attach by threading ribbon through hole in tag. Glue ribbon on back of tag. Glue fibers and hexagon on tag and attach pin to back.

by Tim Holtz

Imagine Card

MATERIALS: 5½" x 8½" Green notecard • 2½" x 6¼" piece of Black matboard • 3½" x 6¼" piece of White paper • Bravissimo papers (5¼" x 8¼" Copper, 4½" x 7½" Gold print) • 4" square and 4¾" x 7¾" piece of Black paper • Wood scrabble tiles • Friendly plastic (Gold, Copper, Metallic Blue) • 12 Copper and 4 Black eyelets • Alcohol ink • AMACO face push mold • Assorted colored wires • Blue Moon glass beads • Quick-Grab glue
INSTRUCTIONS: Heat Friendly Plastic in water and mold faces. Color White paper with alcohol ink. Glue faces on paper. Cut Black matboard to frame faces and glue in place. Use eyelets to attach layered Bravissimo papers and 4¾" x 7¾" Black paper to card. Punch holes in matboard and set eyelets. Thread wires through eyelets and attach glass beads around faces. Glue scrabble tiles on Black paper and trim leaving narrow borders. Glue tiles on card.

by Tim Holtz
The Shower

Okay, so maybe I got a little out of control with this one, but what fun... I decided to use eyelets in a way I have never seen, so why not a shower? MATERIALS: Wood frame with 5½" x 6¾" opening • Red matboard to cover back of frame • 5" x 6¼" piece of Yellow marble matboard • 5" x 6" piece of thin vinyl • White cardstock • 14 Silver eyelets • Rose and bathtub rubber stamps • Black Decor-It ink • Red and Green markers • 12 Silver jump rings • Thin aluminum rod • 24 gauge Silver wire • Diamond Glaze • Tiny glass marbles • Small watering can • Scrap of terry cloth • ⅛" hole punch

INSTRUCTIONS: Stamp roses on thin vinyl and color backs with markers. Attach eyelets along top of vinyl. Slip jump rings through eyelets and thread onto aluminum rod. Insert eyelets in top corners of marble matboard and attach rod with wire. Stamp bathtub on cardstock and additional bubbles on cardstock. Accent some bubbles with Diamond Glaze and add glass marbles while glaze is still wet. Remove end of spout from watering can for shower head. Cut two 4" pieces of rod for shower pipe. Glue the pipe and shower head on matboard. Shape and glue tub and bubbles in place. Glue towel on tub. Attach the Red matboard to back of frame and glue tub scene in place.

Tub & Suds Patterns

The Shower
by Tim Holtz

Create a charmingly whimsical piece of wall art for your bath with metal pieces, vinyl and paper!

Jewelry with Eyelets

by Gail Ellspermann

1. Wipe color across shapes with ink pad.

Eyelets, matboard and beads are the main ingredients for this tastefully stylish jewelry collection!

Bracelet Closure

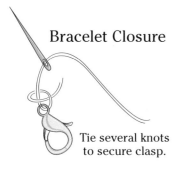

Tie several knots to secure clasp.

String beads and eyelets as shown. Tie several knots to secure jump ring to end.

Overhand Knot

Scarlet & Silver Bracelet

MATERIALS: 32 Red eyelets • 17 Silver E beads • 16 Red 6mm disk beads • Silver clasp • Silver jump ring • 48" of Nymo thread • Needle • Diamond Glaze

INSTRUCTIONS: Fold thread in half and thread fold through needle so you have 4 strands of thread. Securely tie strands to clasp making several knots to secure. Place a drop of glaze on knot for extra hold. String beads and eyelets as shown, repeating pattern until bracelet is desired length. Attach jump ring to end. Tie several knots to secure. Place a drop of glaze on knot, trim thread after glaze dries.

Crystal & Eyelet Bracelet

MATERIALS: 20 Purple eyelets • 10 Crystal star beads • 29 Pink lined Clear E beads • Silver clasp • Silver jump ring • 24" of Silamide thread • Diamond Glaze

INSTRUCTIONS: Fold thread in half and bead with 2 strands. Securely tie thread to clasp making several knots secure. Place drop of glaze on knot for extra hold. Silamide thread is stiff enough to bead without a needle. String beads and eyelets in order shown, repeating pattern until bracelet is desired length. Attach jump ring to end. Tie several knots to secure. Place a drop of glaze on knot, trim thread after glaze dries.

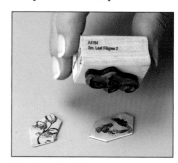

2. Apply foil and stamp designs.

3. Finish the edges with foiling pen.

4. Punch the holes and attach eyelets.

5. Attach the shapes with jump rings.

Leaf Necklace

MATERIALS: Matboard • *Impression Obsession* small leaf rubber stamp • Multi-color metal leaf • Leafing adhesive • Gold leafing pen • Small paintbrush • Ink (Sage, Mandarin, Saffron) • Black permanent ink • 20 leaf beads • Jump rings • 1/8" hole punch

INSTRUCTIONS: Cut matboard into 21 small random shape beads. Using direct-to-paper method, color 7 pieces with each color ink. Use small paintbrush to apply leafing adhesive to each matboard bead. Apply metal leaf when glue becomes tacky. After drying, use Black ink to stamp small leaf image on each matboard bead. Finish edges with Gold leafing pen. Punch a hole in each end of each bead. Insert and set eyelets. Slip jump ring in end of each bead. Open another jump ring, slip on a matboard bead, leaf bead, then another matboard bead. Close jump ring. Continue until all beads and leaves are strung together.

Leaf Bracelet

MATERIALS: Gold clasp • 5 leaf beads

INSTRUCTIONS: Make 6 matboard beads and assemble bracelet following necklace instructions. Attach clasp to one end.

Leaf Earrings

MATERIALS: 2 Gold ear wires • 4 leaf beads

INSTRUCTIONS: Make 4 matboard beads following necklace instructions. Attach beads and ear wires with jump rings referring to photo.

Jump ring Tip

Open and close jump ring using needle-nose pliers.

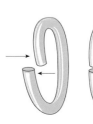

by Sheila Cunningham

Sheila Cunningham is a freelance photographer and artist working in photography, book arts and block printing. She also designs paper art and craft projects. In addition to commerical work and commissions, she teaches classes and workshops.

Leaf Card & Envelope

by pj dutton

MATERIALS: Black and Silver cardstock • Silver and Black eyelets • Silver washers • Cord or ribbon • Pressed leaves cube rubber stamp • Platinum Planet ink • Envelope template • Circle punches (⅛", ½" and 1") • Score tool • Double-stick tape

INSTRUCTIONS: Cut envelope using template and punch holes. Stamp random leaf images. Score and fold lines on envelope. Punch two ½" circles from Black cardstock and two 1" circles from Silver cardstock. Punch ⅛" holes in center of circles. Stack larger circle, small circle, Silver washer, then Black eyelet and attach to bottom flap of envelope. Repeat on top flap. Tie cord under top circle. Stamp leaf on 2" square of Black cardstock. Position on 3" square of Silver cardstock, punch holes and attach with Silver eyelets. Position Silver piece on Black card front, punch holes and attach with Black eyelets.

Tag Book

MATERIALS: Black cardstock • 5½" x 7½" piece of Black cardstock • Two 1⅝" x 5¼" pieces of Black decorative paper • 3¾" x 5½" piece of Black cardstock • 2 *Jean Ruggles* tag rubber stamps • Iridescent ink pad • Metallic paint pens • Bronze seed beads • Crystal E beads • 8 pieces of 8" Black linen thread • 10 Black eyelets • 3¾" x 5½" piece of Silver paper • Asst. small circle punches • Two 1¼" squares of aluminum tape

INSTRUCTIONS: Stamp 3 large circle tags and 4 small Iridescent tags on Black cardstock and let dry. Cut out and trim with metallic paint pens. Set eyelet in top of each tag. Tie one end of linen thread in eyelets of all tags. Score and fold 5½" x 8½" Black cardstock 1⅞" from one short side and 2⅜" from opposite short side. Score and fold ¼" from each of these folds. Cut two 1⅝" x 5¼" decorative paper panels and attach to front panels on card. Cut two ¾" circles and two 1¼" diameter circles of Black cardstock. Cut two 1¼" diameter circles of aluminum tape. Draw designs on aluminum tape with pen and stick on 1¼" Black circles. Stack ¾" circle on top of each Silver circle. Punch hole in center of stacked circles. Center on front panel, mark and punch front panel. Insert and set Black eyelet through circle and right front panel. On left, mark and punch hole. Slip end of linen thread through hole, place Black circles on top and set Black eyelet. To close card, wrap linen thread between circles. Open front panels, punch various size circles in back panel. Set Black eyelet at center top. Gather threads of all tags and secure through eyelet. Let tails of thread hang in front of panel. Add beads to tails. Glue decorator paper on back of panel. Finish back with 3¾" x 5½" piece of Black cardstock.

S mall purses and clever cards are dramatic in metallic colors.

Journal Book Purse

MATERIALS: 6½" x 11" Black cardstock • 2" x 4¾" Black cardstock • Five 5½" x 8½" Black text weight sheets • 3" x 10" Black text weight paper • *Rubber Gems* Large alphabet stamp • Assorted Iridescent ink pads • 8 Black eyelets • Four 16" lengths of decorative fibers • 7" and two 12" pieces of ¼" Black ribbon • 5" of beaded fringe • Alphabeads to spell journal • Self-adhesive Velcro

INSTRUCTIONS: Score and fold 6½" x 11" Black cardstock 1" from short side then 5" from that fold. Orient paper so that 1" tab is on right side in front of you. Ink large alphabet stamp with iridescent inks & stamp on both 5" sections of folded cardstock. Let dry. Punch 3 evenly spaced holes in each fold.

To add top cuff, score and fold 2¼" from long side of 3" x 10" Black text weight paper, fold in half matching short sides together. Tear along side opposite score line to make jagged edge. With 1" tab on right, attach Black text paper to top of purse by folding over and gluing. Insert and set an eyelet in each top corner. Tie knot in one end of one 12" ribbon leaving a tail. Thread through one front eyelet going from outside to inside, leave enough for handle and thread back through other side going from inside to outside, tie knot in one end of ribbon leaving tail. Repeat on back. On front Black strip, set Black eyelets 1" from top and ¾" from each side, then ½" from those eyelets. Thread ribbon through eyelet on one side, tie knot to secure on outside leaving short tail. Come out second eyelet and thread on beads, going in through third eyelet and out last eyelet. Tie knot to secure on outside leaving short tail.

To make inside book, fold text weight sheets in half and stack. Mark and punch holes in book to align with folds. Sew book into fold of purse Start with top hole and thread 2 decorative fibers from outside to inside leaving tail, go back out center hole, down spine to bottom hole, back to inside, out center hole and up to top hole. Adjust thread so tails are even and tie off. Sew opposite side same way. Glue fringe on inside of back cover. Add 2" x 4¾" pocket of Black cardstock adhering on bottom and outside edge and hiding raw edge of fringe. Attach pieces of Velcro to 1" tab and back panel for closure.

Triangle Flap Fringed Card Holder

MATERIALS: Two 4" x 6½" pieces of Black cardstock • Two 4" x 6½" pieces of complementary decorative papers • 9½" x 6¼" piece of Black cardstock • 5½" x 8" & 5¼" x 8" pieces of complimentary decorative papers • 22 Bronze eyelets • 10" of beaded fringe • Two 36" Black ribbons • Glue

INSTRUCTIONS: Cut two rectangles with triangle flaps from 4" x 6½" Black cardstock. Score and fold 1" from long side. Score two 4" x 6½" decorative papers ½" from long side and then again ½" from first score. Trim one decorative paper ⅛" smaller than flap. Trim other decorative paper ¼" smaller than flap. Layer trimmed decorative papers on one Black flap. On 6¼" x 9½" Black cardstock, score and fold ½" on one short edge. Then score and fold 4⅛" from the first fold. On the other short end, score and fold 4⅛" from that edge.

Center and layer 5½" x 8" & 5¼" x 8" decorative papers on outside of folded Black cardstock leaving tab uncovered. Set 5 eyelets, centered and evenly spaced on sides of front and back. Glue the ½" tab on Black cardstock triangle flap under tab of card holder. Glue fringe on triangle flap. Glue other triangle flap with decorated papers on top of this letting ½" of papers adhere to back of card holder.

Set eyelets on either end of tab on top. Lace up sides by starting one ribbon on the front and one on the back with knots on the outside. Slip both ribbons through the eyelet on top, leave a loop for handle, go back through other eyelet on opposite end and continue down side knotting at the end.

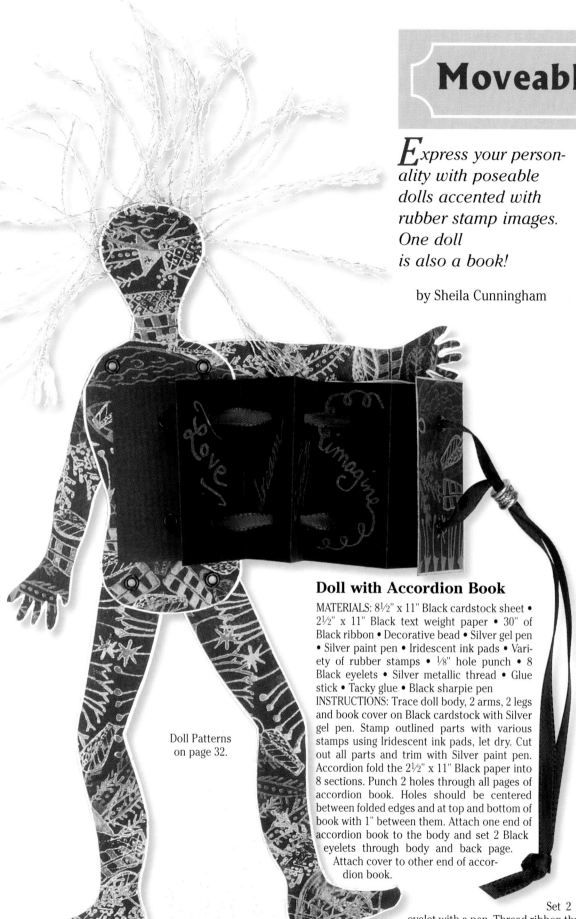

*E*xpress your person-
*ality with poseable
dolls accented with
rubber stamp images.
One doll
is also a book!*

by Sheila Cunningham

1. Trace and stamp design
on doll parts.

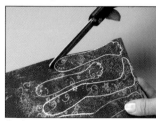

2. Cut out stamped pieces.

3. Fold book and add let-
tering with Silver pen.

4. Attach book to body
with eyelets.

5. Thread ribbon through
the pages of the book.

Doll Patterns
on page 32.

Doll with Accordion Book

MATERIALS: 8½" x 11" Black cardstock sheet •
2½" x 11" Black text weight paper • 30" of
Black ribbon • Decorative bead • Silver gel pen
• Silver paint pen • Iridescent ink pads • Variety of rubber stamps • ⅛" hole punch • 8
Black eyelets • Silver metallic thread • Glue
stick • Tacky glue • Black sharpie pen
INSTRUCTIONS: Trace doll body, 2 arms, 2 legs
and book cover on Black cardstock with Silver
gel pen. Stamp outlined parts with various
stamps using Iridescent ink pads, let dry. Cut
out all parts and trim with Silver paint pen.
Accordion fold the 2½" x 11" Black paper into
8 sections. Punch 2 holes through all pages of
accordion book. Holes should be centered
between folded edges and at top and bottom of
book with 1" between them. Attach one end of
accordion book to the body and set 2 Black
eyelets through body and back page.
Attach cover to other end of accordion book.

Set 2 Black eyelets. Touch up back of
eyelet with a pen. Thread ribbon through all pages of book going from
front to back, across back of doll to other eyelet and back through to front.
Extend accordion book to its full length, thread both ends of ribbon through bead
and tie knot. Attach arms and legs with Black eyelets. Punch small holes around head, insert
Silver metallic thread and tie a double knot. Trim to desired length. If knots need securing, add
a drop of glue from the back.

by pj dutton

Time Dancer

MATERIALS: Ultra Creme and Black cardstock • *Stampers Anonymous* rubber stamps (Mistress of the Hour, synchronicity, clock collage)• Coal ink • Gold ink • Assorted colored pencils • Diamond Glaze • Gold eyelets • Craft knife • Double-stick tape • Gold gel pen
INSTRUCTIONS: Stamp images on Creme cardstock using Coal ink. Color as desired. Coat thinly with glaze. Let dry. Cut out parts with craft knife. Assemble using eyelets. Stamp clock collage on Black card front using Gold ink. Draw line at top and bottom of card with gel pen. Attach doll to card using small piece of double stick tape at center of body. Allow arms, legs and head to move.

Queen of the Games

MATERIALS: Cardstock (Ultra Creme, Baby Blue, Chili Red, Black) • Coal and Cobalt Blue ink • Assorted colored pencils • Craft knife • Diamond Glaze • Blue eyelets • 1/8" hole punch • *Stampers Anonymous* Lady Luck and game card rubber stamps
INSTRUCTIONS: Stamp lady luck parts and game card on Creme cardstock using Coal ink. Color images with pencils as desired. Coat colored images with a thin coat of glaze and let dry. Cut out pieces with craft knife. Assemble paper doll using game card as the body. Punch holes and attach parts using eyelets. Stamp Baby Blue cardstock with random Cobalt Blue game card images. Trim Blue and Black layers of cardstock and attach to card front with double stick tape. Attach paper doll to card front with double-stick tape on center of body. Allow arms, legs and head to move freely.

by Leigh Edwards for Limited Edition Stamps

Yellow Doll

MATERIALS: White cardstock • Assorted *Limited Edition* rubber stamps • Rainbow and Black ink pads • 4 Gold 4mm brads • Diamond Glaze 24 gauge Copper wire • Assorted E beads• Craft knife • Black pen • 1/16" hole punch
INSTRUCTIONS: Color cardstock with Rainbow ink pad and stamp Black images. Outline with Black pen Coat thinly with glaze on both sides. Let dry. Cut out parts with craft knife. Assemble using brads. Punch 5 holes in head and attach beads with wire. Wire beads around ankle.

Rainbow Doll

MATERIALS: White cardstock • Assorted *Limited Edition* rubber stamps • Rainbow and Black ink pads • 4 Red 4mm brads • Diamond Glaze • Craft knife • Black pen • 1/16" hole punch
INSTRUCTIONS: Color cardstock with Rainbow ink pad and stamp Black images. Outline with Black pen. Coat thinly with glaze on both sides. Let dry. Cut out parts with craft knife. Assemble using brads.

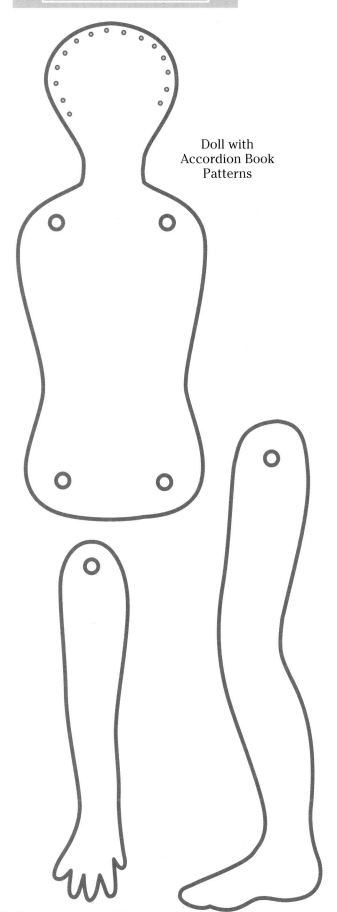

Doll with
Accordion Book
Patterns

Postal Art
by Limited Edition Stamps

Leigh Edwards owns Limited Edition Rubber Stamps. She is an occasional artist whose work has been published in magazines and books.

Michael D' Angelo's Hands

MATERIALS: Cardstock (Tan, Black, White) • Old newspaper page • *Limite Edition* rubber stamps (Michael D' Angelo's Hands, Pieces of Old and Girl face) • Mini word tiles • Lamp Black and Brown ink pads • Sponge • 8mr brads • 1/16" hole punch • Glue stick
INSTRUCTIONS: Cut 4" x 5½" piece of Brown cardstock. Tear piece of newspape into uneven rectangle. Sponge edges of newspaper with Brown ink. Stamp Blac hands on White cardstock, trim to 2" x 3" and sponge edges Brown. On separat piece of White cardstock, stamp Black Pieces of Old. Cut out face section, spong edges Brown and mount on trimmed Black cardstock. Glue newspaper section t Brown card. Glue White card on newspaper. Glue face so fingers are touching i Edge Inspiration tiles edge with Brown, mount on Black cardstock and glue to to of card. Punch a hole in each corner of card and insert brads.

Ta Fin

MATERIALS: Tan and Grey cardstock • Prussian Blue, Moss Green and Lam Black ink pads • *Limited Edition* rubber stamps (Ta Fin, Paris R. Bonapart Paris a Brest, Pirosgafi, Ta Fin Faux Postage Stamp) • 8mm Brass brads • Glu stick • 1/16" hole punch
INSTRUCTIONS: Cut 4¼" x 5½" piece of Tan and 4½" x 5¾" piece of Gre cardstock. Using Black ink, stamp all 4 images on Tan card. Glue Ta Fin fau postage stamp on Tan card. Randomly sponge with Blue and Green. Mount Ta card on Grey cardstock. Punch holes in corners. Attach brads through holes

Charming little postage stamp designs adorn these cards and box. The muted colors give an antique look.

1. Glue squares on front of the card.

2. Punch holes in corners for brads.

3. Insert brads and secure by bending legs.

Pelicos Box

1. Make hole through eyelet opening.

2. Hammer brads into place on box.

Pelicos Box

by Leslie Stewart

MATERIALS: 7½" x 9" wood cigar box • 2⅛" x 7" piece of thin balsa wood • Paint (Metallic Bronze, Russet, Black, Metallic Olive Green) • Limited Edition rubber stamps • Dye Inks (Caramel, Butterscotch, Mushroom) • Black ink pad • Ranger ink (Raisin, Denim, Lettuce, Caramel) • Black pigment ink • Black and Gold embossing powder • Gold pigment • Black 24 gauge wire • Mica sheet • 4 small screw eyes • 4 Brass brads • 8 eyelets • Plastic screw top dime coin tube • Vials with corks • Aluminum, glass topped bead containers • Mini Altoid tin • Glitter and embossing powders • Assorted found objects including stones, seeds, shells and feathers

PAPER: Two 4" x 6" manila envelopes • Small coin envelope • Scrap of cardstock • Assorted tags • Computer generated letter and address labels • Torn piece of map • Matchbox • Rusted tin top paper box • Assorted decorative papers

TOOLS & SUPPLIES: Sandpaper • Craft knife • Stamp • T-pin • Small tack hammer • Toothpicks • Foam paintbrush • Heat gun • E6000 glue • Tacky glue • Paper adhesive

INSTRUCTIONS: Sand the box and remove any paper. Stain Metallic Russet, highlight Metallic Bronze and Black. Stamp images on box with Black pigment ink and emboss with Black powder.

Glue balsa wood divider inside box. Paint mini Altoid tin, aluminum parts of bead containers, vial corks and caps Metallic Olive, Black and Russet. Paint screw eyes Black and lizard Green. To age paper pieces, crumple, tear, stain, and color with dye inks using a cotton ball. Stamp and emboss Black image on packing envelope. Stamp the postal images and cut out with stamp scissors. Stamp letters and numbers on the tags. Insert eyelets in corners of packing envelopes. Emboss Gold images on the mica sheet.

ASSEMBLY: Tie round tag through lower right eyelet on packing envelope with wire. Glue postal images, packing envelope and address labels as shown. Nail brads through eyelet holes in packing envelope. Insert letter in packing envelope. Make hinge stop with screw eyes and wire. Fill and cap containers. Arrange boxes, containers and found objects as desired and glue in place.

Diva Dolls
by Stephanie Jones Rubiano

*W*hether time is flying or passing gently, you'll enjoy these dolls. Make them for yourself and l as gifts for special friends.

Stephanie Jones Rubiano *is a studio artist who has taught stamping, paper crafting and polymer clay classes. Her work has graced the pages of several magazines and sells in stores and galleries all around the United States.*

Metal 'Paper' Dolls

MATERIALS: Decorative papers • 1/8" eyelets • Assorted Rubber stamps • Thin Copper sheet • 24 gauge wire • Small crystals or charms • MultiSnips scissors • Crafter's ink • Metallic Krylon pen • Clear acrylic sealer • Hand held metal punch • 2-hole metal punch • Craft knife • Nylon hammer • Metal file • Sharpie pen • Ultimate glue

INSTRUCTIONS: With pen, trace around arm and leg patterns on thin copper sheet. Note: You can enlarge or reduce templates to customize size of finished doll. Carefully cut out the pieces with snips. Cut edges are very sharp. File edges and use nylon hammer to flatten the metal if it warps during the cutting.

For body, cut a rectangle with circle on top (using patterns) or use your favorite rubber stamps to design a body. Stamp image on scratch paper and use it as a template when creating the new design. Collage pieces for arms, legs and body using thin paper. You can create your own paper designs with rubber stamps. Heat set inks before collaging. Carefully spread glue on back of papers and press onto metal pieces. Set aside and let dry. Trim off any excess paper with a craft knife. Edge pieces with metallic pen if desired. Spray pieces with Clear acrylic sealer and let dry. Punch 1/8" holes in all of pieces. Assemble arms and legs by placing and securing eyelets in elbow and knee joints. Attach arms and legs to body with eyelets at shoulder and hip joints. For hair, punch 1/16" holes in head, loop 24 gauge wire twice through holes and curl around pen. Glue small crystals or charms to doll.

1. Cut out pattern and trace shape on copper.

2. Carefully cut out pieces. The metal is sharp.

3. Cut body from copper using rubber stamp for pattern.

4. Cut out and glue paper to copper pieces.

5. Punch holes and assemble piece with eyelets.

6. Attach arms and legs to body at shoulder and hips.